THE PATH TO INNER PEACE

A Guide to Healing Childhood Trauma

Author

Bob publication

World Vision Ltd.

PROMOTING THE CONTINUED WORK OF GROWTH

This book is not intended to replace or stop any work, growth or content but rather to promote growth and success. We believe this book is a valuable resource and hope our interpretation and commentary will encourage more people to discover and engage with it.

Introduction

As many as one billion children worldwide between the ages of 2 and 17 have been subjected to some form of physical, emotional, or sexual abuse or neglect, as stated by the Global Prevalence of Past-year Violence Against Children 2019 report. If you are one of them, I want you to know that I am here to help you and that, as a therapist, I understand what you are going through. Confronting the pain you endured as a child directly from a traumatic experience is challenging but necessary. Your recurring nightmares and flashbacks may result from unresolved traumatic stress symptoms, especially if you've avoided remembering upsetting childhood events. Your childhood traumatic experiences could be the root cause of your panic attacks. You may experience more bouts of depression since you can't seem to let go of the terrible things that occurred to you when you were a child. Any one of these stages of development in a child's life has the potential to leave an impression on them, regardless of their age. Children subjected to traumatic experiences may be affected in ways that, if not treated, may last for the rest of their lives. It's possible that you are not even aware of the effects trauma has on you, just like this person who survived trauma: " After parking my car, I started walking in the direction of the shopping center while covering my swollen eyes with a pair of dark sunglasses. When I finally broke down and cried, I had just walked out of a therapy session. We concluded that I treat virtually every aspect of life as if it were a form of punishment for myself. As I walked across the parking lot, the only thing going through my head was, "How could I not see it? How is it possible for me to be so oblivious to the thoughts I have and the actions I take to control myself? Am I a masochist who acts without conscious awareness but has no idea what I'm doing? I ought to be able to perform better than this!

Given that one of my coping mechanisms was engaging in self-sabotage, berating myself for not performing to a higher standard was not the best course of action. This time, I could identify it, and I had one of the most profound epiphanies regarding the effects that my traumatic experience has had on my life due to that realization. It was terrifying, but at the same time, it gave me a sense of freedom.

When we are taught as children that we are not deserving of much, or at least not much good stuff, we will unconsciously undermine everything that creates hope for a better future. This is because we will believe that we are not deserving of much. Because our subconscious is hardwired to confirm any self-limiting thoughts we may have, our self-destructive habit can thrive. You may be experiencing the effects of traumatic stress if your memories of a violent event, such as physical, emotional, or sexual abuse or other types of childhood trauma, interfere with your daily functioning. If this happens, you should address these issues as soon as possible. It is possible that undiagnosed post-traumatic stress disorder will cause you to experience undesirable emotional reactions, such as lashing out at people in interpersonal relationships, and you may be unsure of why this is happening to you. As you delve deeper, you realize that the emotional wounds you suffered as a child still affect you and that you are reliving those traumatic experiences in your adult life. Your injuries will not begin to heal until you can openly discuss the trauma caused by the physical or sexual abuse you experienced as a child. As a child who was a domestic violence victim, you might feel guilt or shame about what happened to you. These are all perfectly natural feelings, but they won't help you overcome the hurtful things that have happened to you. Fortuitously, many adults resort to unhealthy coping mechanisms, such as substance abuse, to manage the feelings associated with child-traumatic stress. To begin healing from the wounds caused by your childhood, you must face your history and work to mitigate the effects of the traumatic stress you experienced as a child. You do not have to go through this ordeal by yourself. I will always be here for you.

Worksheets that are tailored to the needs of adults who suffered traumatic experiences as children are included in this book. The book is divided into two parts, the first of which discusses the various ways you may have been abused as a child and how this abuse manifests itself in adulthood through your routines, thought patterns, and behavior. Worksheets are included in the second section of the book. They are designed to assist you in recognizing and comprehending negative emotions and thoughts, dealing with unhealthy habits and patterns, letting go, feeling worthy, authentic, and happy, and moving forward with your life. As a therapist with nine years of experience, I drew from that experience and my professional knowledge to develop this book. Daily, I work with patients who have P.T.S.D. (Post-Traumatic Stress Disorder), and many of those patients experienced some traumatic event during their childhood. Worksheets included in this book are the ones I have used with patients and found to be extremely helpful and practical. It is time for you to start healing from the trauma you experienced. Let's get started.

Chapter 1

It is not Impossible; it is just hard to do what you desire.

The experiences during the first few years of a person's life significantly impact how the brain matures and forms a person's emotions, intelligence level, and personality. Whether or not an infant or child will lay a strong foundation for their future social and emotional health is significantly influenced by whether or not they have positive interactions with members of their family, caregivers, and the larger community. They also help the child's developing brain to mitigate the potential adverse effects of abuse or neglect on their development. According to studies, infants and children can learn more and make essential connections in their developing brains when the primary caregivers in their lives make them feel loved and safe. When a child is afraid or feels threatened, their brains automatically switch into a mode that helps them survive. Brain imaging studies have shown that children with documented abuse have significant structural and functional alterations in their brains. [Citation needed] These studies show that traumatic experiences, such as abuse, neglect, and other forms of stress, can change the brain in negative ways that can last for a person's entire lifetime. Children who go through traumatic experiences are at an increased risk of developing a "heightened stress response." This can hurt their ability to control their emotions, impair their immune system function, cause sleeping problems, and increase the likelihood of developing various medical disorders as they age. Those who have endured childhood abuse experience negative emotions, including guilt, fear, shame, helplessness, worry, grief, anger, and despair. Adults who suffered traumatic experiences or abuse as children have increased rates of depression, anxiety, self-harm, post-traumatic stress disorder, suicidal ideation, substance abuse, and problems in their relationships. Let's get deep into it.

1.1 What is Your Childhood Trauma?

Even though it is commonly believed that children are incredibly resilient and capable of recovering from almost any scenario, traumatic experiences during childhood can have severe and long-lasting impacts that endure far into adulthood if they are not addressed. These effects can continue to impact a person even if the experiences are not addressed. Childhood trauma can be caused by anything that strips a child of their sense of control and alters their perception of safety and security, including but not limited to sexual, physical, or verbal abuse; an unstable or unsafe environment; domestic violence; parental separation; neglect; bullying; life-threatening illness; or invasive medical procedures. A child may experience trauma as a result of any experience in which they perceive that they are in a particularly frightening, dangerous, or overwhelming situation. Children who go through traumatic experiences feel helpless and terrified in ways that are well beyond their capacity for mental and emotional processing. These feelings can last long after the event has passed. These conditions may be the result of recurrent incidents of physical, sexual, or verbal abuse, or they may be the result of one-time events such as accidents or natural disasters. All of these occurrences have the potential to inflict emotional and psychological trauma on children, the effects of which can last well into adulthood in some cases. There is a good chance that everyone's experience of childhood trauma will be unique, but there are a few key events that appear to have the most long-lasting effects on those of us who were unlucky enough to witness them:

1. Physical abuse occurs when someone or something that has power over you uses that power to cause you to suffer physical harm. Injuries in this category include cuts, scratches, bruises, burns, broken bones, and even loss of consciousness.

2. The manipulation of someone's emotions constitutes abuse, even though we do not typically think of it this way. If someone intentionally causes you to lose your emotional equilibrium or sense of dignity, they abuse you. The most common forms of emotional abuse are those in which the victim is

threatened, humiliated, made the target of scapegoating, confined, or coerced into inflicting harm upon themselves.

3. When our caretakers fail to provide us with the things we need to survive physically, such as food, clothing, or a place to live, this is an example of neglect known as physical neglect.

4. Sexual abuse is one of the most damaging forms of child abuse and, sadly, one of the most common forms. The National Center for Victims of Crime estimates that approximately one in five girls and one in twenty boys will be the victims of childhood sexual abuse at some point in their lives; however, these numbers are typically higher because of the low reporting rate. This makes it one of the most common causes of childhood trauma.

5. The neglect of a child's emotional needs is a severe problem, but it is also one of the most challenging problems for adults to acknowledge and accept. If your caregiver does not provide you with the necessary care and connection for you to thrive, then they are guilty of emotionally neglecting you.

6. The death of a parent or other primary caregiver is a harrowing experience for children of any age. The effects will remain long after you are barely old enough to remember what happened to you. After the death of a parent, it's not always easy to grasp how frail we can become emotionally and psychologically.

7. Natural disasters: Although being affected by a natural disaster is upsetting for everyone, young children and children who are still growing find being in these situations excruciatingly painful. Natural disasters such as fires, floods, and hurricanes can cause trauma in various unexpected ways.

Trauma does not discriminate; anyone can experience it at any time. On the other hand, if it happens to us when we are younger, it can cause us a great deal of harm. If you suffered a traumatic experience as a child, the fact that the problems you overcame when you were younger still give you trouble might surprise you. You might be worried that the traumatic experiences you had as a child will negatively affect your happiness, relationships, or even your professional prospects in some way. It's possible that you don't know where to start when it comes to learning how to heal. You have not been feeling like yourself as of late, have you? You have been curious whether you have any unresolved traumatic experiences from your childhood. You had the impression that it was over. On the other hand, the traumatic experiences you endured as a child might carry over into your adult life and make you feel as though your world is turned upside down. If that is the case, then why now?

The question "Why now?" seems to be worth sixty million dollars to answer. You have made an effort to get better and have even successfully avoided the problem on multiple occasions. But recently, you've noticed that your anxiety has returned, bringing you to the verge of having panic attacks occasionally. A predominant sense of melancholy is beginning to take hold. You might even have the urge to crawl into a hole and hide. This is unhealed trauma from the past. Let's figure out how this impacts your life right now.

1.2. In what ways does it make you feel?

As many of us already know, research conducted over several years has proven that childhood traumatic experiences negatively impact our emotional, psychological, and even physical well-being. The many forms of emotion dysregulation and stress reactivity linked to childhood trauma are thought to be one of the connections between childhood trauma and physiological illnesses. Several studies have supported this theory. People who were brought up in emotionally abusive environments are at a greater risk of developing more severe stress reactions and more interpersonal problems than adults. These impacts continue to show up in strange ways throughout our adult lives, even though there may be a significant amount of time and space that separates us from the event in question. Learning to recognize the symptoms of problematic childhood experiences is essential to our recovery, although doing so may be difficult at times.

• Conducting Oneself in a Passive-Aggressive Manner

Adults who overcame traumatic experiences as children frequently carry a significant amount of pent-up rage within them that they cannot control. They choose to ignore these challenging emotions rather than deal with them head-on. As a result, they engage in passive-aggressive behavior that has the potential to alienate them and damage meaningful relationships. These individuals frequently use sarcasm, which they excuse by claiming it's humor or "mistakes," which they insist were not done on purpose. They are concerned about the consequences that may result from expressing their rage. As a result, they do not consider it to be a safe option. Instead, to protect their already-repaired hearts, they engage in behavior that could be described as passive-aggressive.

• Capabilities of thought that are diminished

Children who are regularly subjected to either physical or emotional abuse or who are neglected are more likely to have cognitive problems. Problems with memory, poor linguistic skills, and an inability to focus or concentrate on tasks are all conditions that could fall into this category.

• Serial Monogamy

A person is considered a serial monogamist if they minimize their time alone and move as quickly as possible from the end of one relationship to the beginning of another. This is frequently brought on by concerns about receiving another injury, anxieties about being abandoned, or even a desire to make up for the care and love that one did not receive as a child in the hope that one will eventually accept it. Every new person you date allows you to rekindle the belief that you deserve the love and companionship you currently lack.

• Attachment Disorders

If a child suffers a traumatic event between the ages of six months and three years, the child is more likely to have difficulty forming secure bonds with the people who are important to them. You may be unable to create healthy social connections if you have reactive attachment disorder, also referred to as R.A.D. This condition makes it difficult to develop relationships with other people. The only areas of your life in which R.A.D. can affect your feelings and behavior. In addition, it makes it difficult for people who have it to trust others. Then there is the anxious attachment style, characterized by a fear of abandonment. Children who have been neglected or abandoned by a caregiver frequently struggle with abandonment concerns well into adulthood, even if they do not realize it on the surface. This is true even if the child does not learn that they have been neglected or abandoned. Although the underlying concern is that the partner will eventually leave, these thoughts frequently surface in everyday circumstances, such as when a partner leaves the house alone. You find it difficult to calm down or feel anxious about the situation. In more extreme cases, other common manifestations of this fear include feelings of possessiveness or jealousy.

• An inconsistent picture of one's self-concept

This self-concept suggests that you need a clearer understanding of how the thoughts and feelings you are experiencing concerning yourself should be interpreted. [Case in point:] If you cannot differentiate between these feelings and points of view, you may have an inaccurate perspective of who you are or believe that you are "incompatible" with specific classifications of people in society.

• Requiring a Substantial Volume of Space

Children raised in frequently unpredictable or tumultuous environments experience high levels of stress and have hyper-vigilant central nervous systems. Then, when they become adults, they discover that they require a significant amount of time alone to alleviate their anxiety, nervousness, and fear. In extreme circumstances, some people manifest symptoms of social anxiety disorder or even agoraphobia or meet the criteria for either. Being at home, where you have complete command over your setting, not only makes you feel more secure but also allows you to relax and unwind.

• Unsymmetrical Capacity to Regulate One's Behavior

If you are an adult who makes rash decisions, you probably went through a traumatic experience when you were younger. People exposed to traumatic experiences when they were children often struggle to maintain behavioral control as adults. Because they have never been taught how to behave differently, they always act following the emotions they are experiencing. There are a lot of people who are aware of how to do it to get the attention that they would be denied otherwise.

• Continuing to engage in Harmful Relationships

When children grow up in unstable environments with caregivers who struggle with mental or physical illness, drug addiction, or even death, they frequently develop a sense of guilt that stems from wanting to end a connection before being able to "fix" the other person. This sense of responsibility often stems from the child wanting to end the relationship before they can "fix" the other person. Being with someone who isn't a good fit for us can feel safer than being alone at times.

• States of Consciousness That Can Be Altered

A dissociative state can be induced in children (and some adults) when they are subjected to prolonged or recurrent traumatic experiences in childhood. When we are young, we cannot differentiate between the possible states of consciousness; therefore, we are powerless to stop ourselves from entering those states. As a direct consequence of these distorted perceptions of the world, we risk losing touch with our deepest, most authentic selves and the things that give meaning to our lives. Even after so many years, we continue relying on these hallucinatory states to get us through the most trying times.

• Controversies That Are Not Helpful

Conflict is an inevitable part of any partnership. Still, children raised in households where their primary caregivers either constantly argued with one another or actively avoided conflict are less likely to develop the communication skills necessary for effective and healthy communication. Another sign is an ongoing pattern of avoiding or engaging in a conflict within partnerships. This includes the ability to navigate and handle conflict in ways that are healthy and beneficial to oneself and others.

It's possible that they don't know how to make amends after a conflict. When we lack the knowledge of how to manage conflict constructively and healthily, we also lack the knowledge of how to mend a relationship after the inevitable partnership disagreement. This may take the form of denying that the event in question even took place, failing to recognize when or how a compromise could be reached, or remaining silent.

• Being a Victim Over and Over Again

When we were younger, we couldn't understand the factors that led to unfavorable outcomes. Because of this, many of us frequently resort to bizarre or nonsensical thinking to explain away the negative things that occur to us. This behavior continues into adulthood for many of us. When we are forced to develop our identities as victims of abuse or emotional neglect, it isn't easy to consider ourselves as people with no control over their lives. This is especially true when we are forced to develop our childhood identities.

The good news is that you can change these habits and patterns, and you are not doomed to repeat them for the rest of your life. Let's figure out how you can recover from the traumatic experiences you had as a child.

Chapter 2

2.0 Feel

When a child goes through traumatic experiences as a child, they often lose their sense of stability and identity, both of which are detrimental to their sense of self-worth and usually follow them into adulthood. Adults exposed to this traumatic event may still be affected by it, as evidenced by their inability to manage their feelings effectively, their sense of disconnection from others, their elevated levels of anxiety and depression, and their hostility. Now that we better understand our symptoms, let's work on better managing the negative emotions and thoughts connected to our traumatic experience.

2.1. The Ongoing Effects of Previous Trauma

Make a note of the signs and problems that you can identify with or that you have had in the past. Place a checkmark, or an asterisk next to the people or things whose effects you were not aware were a result of your trauma.

How do you feel about yourself now that you know that all of these problems or symptoms directly result from the long-term damage caused by the traumatic event?

2.2. The Unpredictability of My Feelings

Your feelings significantly affect your P.T.S.D. condition and the rest of your life. The goal is to understand your emotions, become aware of them, learn how to control them, and locate appropriate channels through which they can be expressed. Recognize the range of your feelings and take notes on the specifics of your emotional experiences. The following describes some of the emotions associated with traumatic experiences during childhood. Complete the questions at the bottom of the worksheet for each of the feelings discussed.

Despair and a complete lack of hope

Despair and hopelessness are the feelings that come to the surface when you are confronted with unfortunate circumstances, and they leave you with the impression that you have no control over them. You will experience these feelings and feel you are not rooted in life when you are consistently dissatisfied with your life. If you are hopeless, you may stop wishing for better circumstances because you no longer have faith that your situation will improve. You may even decide to end your own life. You may feel that nothing you believe in is worth fighting for and that you should give up.

Anger

Anger is an emotion that arises when a person is aware that they are being attacked or in danger, believes that the world has mistreated them, and believes they have the power to change it. It may involve a severe and antagonistic response to something that is imagined as a threat, an insult, or an injury. Your feelings of rage are connected to your sense of significance, power, and importance.

Sadness

When you lose something fundamental to you, you will typically experience sadness. When you're feeling down, you may become withdrawn and hostile. After that, your grieving process will begin. Going through the motions of mourning can make it easier for you to accept your loss, even though it is challenging. It is not uncommon for people to experience suffering, anxiety, and even other feelings, such as rage, in addition to sadness. After you have finished working through your emotions associated with the loss, you can proceed along your chosen path.

Fear

Fear is one of the most uncomfortable feelings humans experience, but it is indispensable for our capacity to continue living and advancing as a species. Fear is an emotion that you feel when you perceive danger, and this fear, in turn, can cause you to become immobile as a response to a traumatic event.

However, the cultural or historical context in which you live significantly impacts how you experience to dread. Some authorities believe that fear is a natural expression of your desire to survive and protect yourself, but others disagree with this interpretation. A wide variety of distinct feelings can be categorized as dread, and there are several psychological and physical ways that these feelings can be expressed.

Please find below the questions that need to be answered for each of the feelings mentioned above.

1 Describe the feeling of (hopelessness/sadness) that comes to mind when you think back on it.

2 How did you respond to the circumstances that arose? What were you thinking and doing at the time?

3 What inspired you to keep going after that? How did you act?

4 Have you ever noticed that many people are going through the same feeling? How do you carry yourself?

5 How does this feeling influence how you interact with other people?

2.3 Recognizing Triggers and Triggering

Every time you have a nagging feeling that you might be triggered, note your reaction (including your feelings, thoughts, and physical responses), how intense it was, what had been going on in the immediate lead-up, and how you dealt with it. Have you tried to cover it up or chosen to ignore it altogether? Who do you think was at fault, the trigger or yourself? Just observe; do not pass judgment.

____

____

____

____

____

2.4 Your Unwanted Ideas

Intrusive thoughts enter your consciousness frequently without notice or provocation and are distressing, upsetting, or odd. We all experience these ideas occasionally, but for some, they become "stuck" and cause great suffering.

Everyone needs logical reasoning as a crucial component of a robust ego capable of coping with P.T.S.D. symptoms. As you rid your thought process of prejudices, delusions, wishful thinking, and emotional blackmail, your ability to think clearly and make rational judgments will improve. Learning how to control distracting thoughts, visions, and urges is essential. One way to manage unwanted thoughts is to write them down. This worksheet aims to help you identify intrusive thoughts by requiring you to write them down, identify their causes and patterns, and learn coping strategies. Write down your intrusive thoughts and the relevant situation from the previous two weeks.

Triggers

Examine each of the conditions. Exist any parallels between the situations? Depict them. (Even though the circumstances may be vastly different, look for the common element, such as a particular sound, scent, feeling, sight, mood, or word.) These resemblances serve as your triggers.

Why do you have unwanted thoughts? Include everything.

____

____

____

____

____

____

Topics

Examine your distracting thoughts right now. Please place them in the table's left column. Consider them. Are they all about the same topic (injuring others, injuring oneself, misbehaving, being injured by objects or people, etc.)? Insert the subject in the column on the right.

Intrusive Thought(s)	Topics

Triggers, Topics, and Reactions

Complete the following chart with the data collected from the steps mentioned above.

Situation	Intrusive Thought (s)	Trigger(s)	Topic	First Reaction	How I Handled Myself	Rate of Success

Here are some suggestions for dealing with intrusive thoughts.

• Label such thoughts as "intrusive thoughts."

• Remind yourself that these automatic thoughts are not under your control.

• Acknowledge and allow the thoughts to enter your mind. Avoid pushing them away.

• Pause. Allow yourself some time.

• Be prepared for the return of your thoughts.

• Continue doing whatever you were before the intrusive thought appeared, allowing the anxiety to exist.

2.5 Distinguishing the Past from the Present

Understanding when we are safe (but triggered) and in actual danger depends on our ability to recognize when we are reacting to the past.

Knowing when we remember is beneficial. It helps us feel less insane, helpless, afraid, angry, depressed, and hopeless. Complete this worksheet to gain a deeper understanding of what occurs whenever you experience distress.

What Are You Doing Throughout the Day?

What Sensations and Emotions Do You Encounter?

What Belief Appears to Explain Your Current Emotions?

____

____

____

____

____

Do these feelings/thoughts make more sense in the Present or the past?

____

____

____

____

____

I hope these exercises will assist you in addressing your negative emotional responses, unhealthy thoughts, and symptoms of childhood trauma.

Chapter 3

3.0 Deal

Childhood trauma does not always leave physical scars, but it does always leave psychological and emotional scars. These impressions may long-term affect a child's physical and mental health, possibly even into adulthood. Perhaps you were abused as a child, and now, whenever you attempt to complete a task, your inner voice tells you that you are inadequate. If you cannot fall asleep any other way, you may need to rock yourself to sleep in your bed. Or perhaps, hidden behind your constant smile, you suffer from the crippling internal shame that no one ever sees. Include some worksheets for overcoming and coping with issues caused by childhood trauma.

3.1 Your Window of Tolerance

Draw a circle around each symptom of autonomic hyperarousal in your experience, and add any missing signs. Write down the circumstances that induce these distinct states. For example, do you become more agitated in the presence of others or alone? At work, do you operate more within the tolerance range?

Signs of Chronic Hyperarousal

Emotional Overstretch, Impulsivity, Panic, Hypervigilance, Sense of Insecurity, Defensiveness, Rapid-Fire Thoughts, Anger, and

____

____

____

____

____

____

When do I find myself hyper-aroused?

Window of Tolerance

My emotions and responses are manageable. I can think and feel at the same time. My answers are situation-specific and

When do I find myself in the tolerance window?

Signs of Chronic Hyperarousal

Numb, "dead," passive, devoid of energy and emotion, incapable of thought, shut down, disconnected, not present, ashamed, unable to say "no," and...

____

____

____

When do I find myself hyper-aroused?

____

____

____

____

____

____

____

How do you attempt to deal with your hyperarousal? Without passing judgment on yourself, list everything you do to reduce your activity level or prevent your emotions from becoming overwhelming.

____

____

____

____

____

____

____

____

____

3.2 Track Your Relapse Cycle

Assumptions at each phase of the cycle should be recorded. How do you feel when you first stop using unhealthy coping mechanisms? What are the signs that your P.T.S. symptoms are worsening? What signals do you receive when your dangerous impulses return? How do relapses ordinarily occur? And what comes next? Avoid criticizing yourself. Be fascinated and interested in the cycle that has constantly propelled you.

The same cycle may repeat itself when you attempt to adopt new, healthy coping mechanisms because the brain and body prefer to revert to old routines in stressful situations. Document any observations you make while trying to alter trauma-related behaviors.

3.3 Be Glad: The G.L.A.D. Technique

It is intended to help you notice the good things that are all around you but which are often overlooked. "G" stands for thankfulness; "L" stands for something you've learned; "A" stands for something you've accomplished; and "D" stands for something that brings you joy. Even though you may wish to complete the G.L.A.D. worksheet throughout the day, it is most practical to do so at the end of the day. Make copies of this worksheet so you can practice the technique every day for at least three weeks. After three weeks, your "positive awareness" will become ingrained. After three weeks, the worksheet may only need to be utilized once weekly, but you should continue to use it frequently (for example, every Sunday night). Being anxious and depressed increases the importance of practicing "positive mindfulness."

Nonetheless, it should also be a skill that helps you discover daily happiness. Additionally, inform others of the positive attributes you list on your worksheet. Sharing your positive emotions and thoughts makes them much more potent.

G - A thing for which you were thankful today. It can simply be the sunlight or the wholesome meals you consume. Write it below.

Now consider a life-defining aspect, such as a meaningful relationship, children, close friends, or your health. Write it below.

L - A lesson you took away from today. List a joyous discovery you made about yourself today. You may already be aware of it, but it has become more apparent now.

Jot down something you learned today about someone else. Again, you may already be aware of it, but today you were more conscious of this quality.

Jot down a fact you discovered today that piqued your curiosity or increased your awareness of your surroundings.

Jot down something you learned today and how it improved your perception of yourself or the world.

A: Describe one small win you had today. You might believe that achievements must involve large or significant tasks, yet the little things have the biggest impact on your life. You may be trying to achieve a goal like getting in more exercise, eating better, or getting a new job. Achieving even small plans is an accomplishment.

List one accomplishment you made today.

D - An enjoyable moment you had today.

What made you smile or laugh?

Which small thing of beauty did you see today?

Which words did you hear today that made you feel good? A song? A child's voice? A joke?

____

____

____

____

____

Close your eyes and reflect on your day and your writing at this point. For a few minutes, take deep breaths.

Then, recall a pleasant memory from the day. If there is anything you want to remember from this activity, write it down.

____

____

____

____

____

____

____

____

3.4 Reconnect with Your Inner Child Follow the steps below to figure out your beliefs by connecting with your inner self.

1. Consider at least one childhood experience in which you felt neglected or harmed.

2. Create a keyword list based on this information. How was your childhood?

Here are a few instances:

Cold, vicious, dominant, indifferent, overprotective, inconsistent, stringent, unpredictable, selfish, pretentious, moody, arrogant, boisterous, aggressive, and sadistic.

3. Consider common phrases your parents may use, such as "You are to blame for my overwhelming workload," "Wait until your father gets home," "Why can't you be like your sister?" and "You'll never achieve anything."

4. Consider your relationship with your parents and the problematic aspects of it, such as "They argued frequently" or "Dad made all decisions on his own."

5. Consider the negative thoughts that your parents' actions have caused you to have, then attempt to connect with your inner child.

A child who observes their parent in a constant state of stress may internalize the notion that they are a burden.

Use the formula below to discover your limiting beliefs:

"I am__________" or "I am not __________," "I am not allowed to __________" or "I am allowed to __________." "I cannot __________" or "I can __________,"

Below are examples of beliefs you might have:

I am worthless.

I am unwelcome.

I am not important.

I am unlovable.

I am always to blame

I am insufficient

I am powerless

I am so small

I cannot do anything

I am so stupid

I should not feel anything

I am substandard

I am a burden

I am inferior

I am always to blame

I must place others ahead of myself.

Try to maintain a distance from your beliefs. Say to yourself, "The hurt inner child within me is worthless," rather than "I am worthless."

Observe the thought without evaluating it as right, wrong, harmful, or sensible. This will allow you to identify your ideas as opinions.

3.5 My Communication Style.

You can handle disagreement more skillfully if you develop your assertiveness. Using the brief quiz below, you can categorize your actions and attitudes as assertive, passive, aggressive, or passive-aggressive, offering some advice on handling conflicts. Each of these strategies is one that we occasionally employ in various situations. Finding your most often used tactics is the aim of this exercise. Circle the number of the statement that you agree. Ignore the parenthesis code for the time being. They will be explained shortly.

When someone does something I do not like, I typically do not say anything. (P)

I find it challenging to compliment others. (P)

I often "blow up" at other people when I am upset. (A.G.)

I speak up in a controlled manner if I feel I have been maltreated. (A)

I make an effort to be impartial and take into account the opinions of others. (A)

I keep silent and retaliate later if someone does anything I do not like. (P.A.)

When I am in a leadership position, I demand that others follow my instructions. (A.G.)

I frequently use voice-raising tactics to influence others to do what I desire. (A.G.)

It is preferable just to let things go rather than upsetting others. (P)

If I agree to do something but do not want to, I "forget" to do it. People who are in a committed relationship should not dispute. (P)

These exercises will help you develop healthy habits and leave your harmful coping mechanisms and behavior patterns behind.

Chapter 4

4.0 Heal

Even the most loving and attentive parents can damage our sense of self irreparably. After a distressing event, our parents may have rushed in with the best intentions and a desire to prevent us from suffering. When we began to cry, our caretaker reassured us that everything was satisfactory. In reality, negative emotions can be advantageous. When experiencing terrible emotions, we must reflect on why we felt as we did. Or perhaps our parents did not provide us with the necessary love and care and forced us to stop crying when we were injured. In either case, we never learned how to express our emotions effectively. We did not.

Understand that emotions have a predictable beginning, middle, and end and that we will survive. When we cannot feel our feelings, we may perceive all emotions as terrifying. Young people cannot differentiate between their feelings and their "selves." We believe we are our emotions. We are unacceptable if our surfaces are not treated with respect in a particular situation. However, the time has come to sever ties with false beliefs and end your suffering. Let's look at some worksheets to assist you in moving forward and living a happy, fulfilling life.

4.1 Strengthening Your "C" Qualities

Use this worksheet to describe your C attributes and the contexts in which they appear. Consider how you can improve these qualities.

Curiosity

Calm

Compassion

Clarity

Courage

Creativity

Connection

Confidence

4.2 Create a Personal Mission Statement

To live each day to the fullest, you must carefully consider your life objectives and the ideas and values that will guide your daily actions. This worksheet is designed to assist you in creating a personal mission statement, also known as a purpose statement, which can serve as a simple road map for leading a contented and fulfilled life. A personal mission statement imparts clarity and direction. It determines your identity and lifestyle. A personal mission statement summarizes your priorities, values, and beliefs in one or two sentences. Individual purpose statements are distinct from setting goals. Your goals are predicated on it. Your daily decisions will be guided by your mission statement, allowing you to decline opportunities that could be distracting. A personal mission statement is a dynamic document that changes over time due to your life experiences. Your mission statement emphasizes both self-discovery and purpose.

To create your mission statement, use this worksheet.

1 Consider the qualities you find significant in the people you admire.

Three people you look up to

____

____

____

____

Qualities you admire that these people possess.

____

____

____

Name five values that best describe you.

2 Consider the parts you play in the lives of your friends, relatives, and coworkers. List all of the significant roles you play in your life.

3 List the most important goals that you would wish to achieve.

4 Think about the person you wish to become, the things you want to be remembered for, and your impact. Write below.

5 Make a list of some of the things you excel.

Your Mission Statement

Write down your mission statement in one or two sentences, including your values, goals, admirable traits, and what you believe to be your life's purpose.

List three ways that you can live out your mission statement every day.

____

____

____

____

____

4.3 Welcome Your Younger Self

Use this worksheet to understand better the child you were at various ages and stages. They are not required to be connected to a particular event, only the environment at that age.

Younger Self

What is this child's age?

What their facial expression and body language are communicating to you?

What is this child's state of mind?

When you see your younger self, notice how you feel toward them.

____

____

____

____

____

____

____

Assume that only a portion of you is responsible for any judgments or negative responses you may have. What do you see regarding this portion?

What happens if you welcome this child as you would any child?

4.4 18% Strategies

This activity focuses on helping you move towards any glimmer of hope.

Any Activity that Gives You even a little bit of Relief

____

____

____

____

What Percent Does It Help?

____

____

____

____

What kind of Feelings, Thoughts, Situations, and Impulse

____

____

____

____

____

4.5 My Self-Esteem

Since you are a human with an innate desire to preserve and survive, your intrinsic value already exists at birth. It is a combination of your skills, characteristics, and flaws.

That is your identity.

Fortunate people are valued and respected for who they are. They do not experience depression or emotional breakdowns in response to criticism. They are eager to develop and improve despite the intense social pressure. However, achievement is built on hard work, personal growth, and overcoming mistakes. People who lack affection and regard have learned to compensate for or overcompensate for their narcissistic wounds. To be admired and appreciated, they must act as if they are someone else: flawless, unbeatable, and always able to win over their audience. Early on, these individuals acquire the skills necessary to adapt to such an abnormal environment. Regardless of how well they manage, their self-esteem becomes exceedingly fragile, inconsistent, and fragile. The necessary scaffolding still needs to be constructed.

Take your time reading the following sentences. Rephrase them so that you perceive the speaker to be overflowing with confidence.

1. I do not feel good about myself when I think about myself. I have difficulty accepting many aspects of myself.

____

____

____

____

____

____

2. I need help to acknowledge the accomplishments and advancement of others. And why should I? Others do not value my achievements or me. They probably do not care.

____

____

____

____

____

____

3. I am conscious of my flaws but must continue pursuing perfection. No matter what I do, I am obese, depressed, and miserable.

4. To earn someone's trust and esteem, I must always play a role. My victories are meaningless, never-ending role-playing games.

5. I must hide my flaws. If I do, someone will take advantage of me right away. I need to maintain my composure at all times.

____

____

____

____

____

____

6. Nothing I do ever measures up. Every new obstacle feels like a trap set up to make me fail.

____

____

____

____

____

____

7. I am unable to satisfy anyone. Why even bother trying?

____

____

8 Imagine being able to see yourself through the loving eyes of your pet as they view you.

What did you experience?

9 What did you think?

Repeat this action several times a week. Bring a picture of that animal with you. Take out the photo of your pet whenever you experience low self-esteem and look at yourself in the pet's eyes.

These exercises will help you move on to a life of satisfaction and love.

Question and Answer Section

Question: What is the significance of addressing childhood trauma on the journey to inner peace?

Answer: Childhood trauma can have a profound impact on a person's life and well-being, affecting their relationships, self-esteem, and ability to cope with stress. Addressing this trauma is crucial in the path to inner peace as it allows individuals to heal from past experiences, overcome negative patterns and beliefs, and cultivate a sense of self-awareness and self-acceptance. By facing and processing their trauma, individuals can release feelings of pain and guilt and ultimately find the inner peace they seek.

Question: How can the principles of mindfulness and self-compassion help in healing childhood trauma?

Answer: The principles of mindfulness and self-compassion can be powerful tools in the healing process of childhood trauma. Mindfulness allows individuals to be present at the moment and observe their thoughts and emotions without judgment. This can help break the cycle of negative thought patterns and provide a sense of control. On the other hand, self-compassion involves treating oneself with kindness and understanding, which can help to build self-esteem and reduce feelings of shame and guilt associated with trauma. By combining mindfulness and self-compassion, individuals can create a safe and supportive inner environment, allowing them to process and heal from their trauma.

What role does therapy play in healing childhood trauma?

Answer: Therapy provides a safe and supportive environment where individuals can process and work through their childhood trauma with the help of a trained professional. With the guidance of a therapist, individuals can work through their trauma in a structured and supportive manner. Therapy can help individuals understand and manage their emotions, develop coping strategies, and gain insight into the impact of their trauma on their lives.

Question: How does the practice of self-reflection aid in the healing process?

Answer: Self-reflection involves reflecting on one's thoughts, feelings, and behaviors. This practice can help individuals understand themselves, identify patterns and beliefs connected to their childhood trauma, and make changes that promote healing. By reflecting on their experiences and emotions, individuals can gain a new perspective and start to release the grip of their trauma on their lives.

Question: Can creative expression be a helpful tool in healing childhood trauma?

Answer: Yes, creative expression can be a powerful tool in the healing process. By expressing themselves through art, writing, music, or other forms of creativity, individuals can process their emotions and gain insight into their experiences in a way that words alone cannot. Creative expression can also provide a sense of catharsis and help individuals release repressed emotions and memories.

Question: Is it necessary to revisit and confront past traumatic experiences to heal?

Answer: Revisiting and engaging past traumatic experiences can be an essential part of the healing process, but it is crucial to approach it in a safe and controlled manner with the guidance of a trained professional. Confronting one's trauma can be difficult and emotional, but it can also lead to a deeper understanding of its impact on one's life and provide closure.

Question: What is the importance of a robust support system in healing childhood trauma?

Answer: A powerful support system can play a crucial role in the healing process of childhood trauma. Having people who are understanding and non-judgmental can provide comfort and encouragement during difficult times. A supportive network can also give a sense of community and help individuals feel less isolated in their healing journey.

Question: Can physical exercise help in healing childhood trauma?

Answer: Yes, physical exercise can be a helpful tool in the healing process. Exercise releases endorphins, which can improve mood and reduce stress. It also provides a healthy outlet for emotions and can be a form of self-care. Engaging in physical activity can also help individuals build confidence and self-esteem, which can be especially important for those who have experienced childhood trauma.

Question: How does spiritual practice fit into the journey to inner peace and healing of childhood trauma?

Answer: Spiritual practice can provide comfort and connection during the healing journey. It can also offer a sense of purpose and meaning and help individuals find peace and comfort in difficult times. Whether through prayer, meditation, or connecting with nature, spiritual practice can be an essential part of the healing process and provide a sense of inner peace.

Question: What role does forgiveness play in the healing of childhood trauma?

Answer: Forgiveness can play a significant role in the healing process of childhood trauma. Forgiving oneself or others can help to release anger, resentment, and guilt and promote peace and closure. However, forgiveness is a personal journey and should only be pursued when individuals are ready and comfortable doing so.

Daily, jot down your questions and provide appropriate responses.

Daily Reflection Questions

What emotions or thoughts related to my childhood trauma came up for me today?

How did I practice self-compassion today?

What did I do to care for myself today?

What is one thing I am grateful for today?

Did I engage in any creative expression today? If so, what did I create?

Did I reach out to my support system today? How did they help me?

Did I engage in any physical activity today? How did it make me feel?

Did I take any time for spiritual practice today? If so, what did I do?

Did I practice mindfulness today? If so, in what ways?

Did I make any progress in my healing journey today? If so, what was the most significant moment?

Conquering Parental Challenges

A Journey Beyond Parental Struggles

Embark on a transformative journey as we navigate and overcome the challenges that come with distant, rejecting, or self-involved parents. Let's break free from the emotional bonds holding us back and soar toward healing and self-discovery.

How The Lives of Adult Children Are Impacted by The Socially Inept Parenting of Their Parents

We are all born with a sentimental financial institution, and when it is depleted due to a lack of positive emotional experiences, we feel emotionally isolated. It can begin in childhood and continue into adulthood.

The pain you experience due to being viewed as invincible by others, particularly those you care about is comparable to physical pain. The only distinction is that it does not manifest physically. Emotional loneliness is characterized by feelings of emptiness in the gut, the belief that no one can understand you, and being alone. This occurs when you do not receive sufficient empathy from others, particularly your caregivers. Emotional closeness is crucial. It involves having someone with whom you can share your life, your burdens, and your emotions. You can be vulnerable with this person and feel safe.

In a relationship, both parties must be emotionally responsive. With it, a connection can be successful. Many people lack self-confidence due to parental rejection. As children, they are emotionally neglected, and they expect the same from others. They need more confidence that everyone will pay attention to them.

Key Element

• Some parents appear to be flawless, have everything you desire, and whom you may secretly wish were your parents; however, they may be emotionally immature. Looks can be deceiving.

Emotional loneliness is felt internally and cannot be seen; therefore, it is easily overlooked.

With self-awareness, you may comprehend the emotional deficiency and how to achieve the necessary change.

• Children who experience emotional loneliness prioritize the needs of others over their own; they do everything to demonstrate they have no emotional needs, which prevents them from forming healthy emotional bonds. They become self-sufficient and mature rapidly. An attentive, dependable, passionate relationship solves a lack of emotional loneliness.

If you grow up with emotionally immature parents, you will experience loneliness. Children who grow up with emotionally immature parents develop a sense of inner emptiness. Even if they have everything they desire, the void remains.

Individuals who experience emotional deprivation as children end up in the same type of relationship or marriage as adults. This is because staying within the familiar is comforting.

Parents who lack emotional maturity are incapable of approving their children's emotions. This causes children to yield to the convictions of others.

Recognition of the Emotional Immigrant's Parent

Because your relationship with your parents is subjective, it is difficult to view them objectively; doing so may feel like betrayal. However, you must be able to do so to comprehend the reasons for their limitations.

Everyone who lacks emotional maturity reacts rashly. They are unaware of how their attitude impacts others. They perceive no wrongdoing in their actions and see no reason to apologize to others. In addition, they never experience regret. As children, many immature people lacked an emotionally intimate and supportive relationship with their parents. They chose to toughen up to endure their emotional isolation. Numerous emotionally immature individuals fear their emotions and find intense, conflicting emotions threatening. They instill in their children a fear of vulnerability.

Typically, emotionally immature people are raised in families where their emotions and intellect are restrained. They develop a simplistic outlook on life and a rigid coping mechanism.

Key Element

Adverse effects can result from emotionally immature parents, particularly in relationships, self-confidence, and self-esteem. This causes them to be overly cautious in their romantic relationships and interactions with others.

How It Feels to Have an Emotionally Immature Parent

Since we share bonds with our parents, growing up with emotionally immature parents is more painful and disappointing. When it comes to accountability and consequences for their actions, whether in the past or the future, emotionally immature parents face a challenge. Emotionally ignorant individuals lack a strong sense of self. In addition, they have an inaccurate perception of family closeness and intimacy. They lack genuine communication due to their lack of empathy and reluctance to build bridges or repair relationships. They cannot be sensitive to others. They are preoccupied with the perception others have of them and argue that their anxiety trumps others regardless of who they are.

Key element.

Our first attachments are to our parents and family members. Even if we reach out to others for various reasons, we always return to our parents to form bonds with them. In relationships, emotional immaturity is the easiest to detect. When it occurs within a parent-child relationship, the consequences can be devastating. If you grew up with emotionally immature parents, communication is nearly impossible. This means that communication is typically unidirectional, and only one person is the center of attention. Some children of emotionally immature parents are unable to express their anger. They can deny it, repress it, or turn it against themselves. They act out their emotional needs rather than tell them verbally. They make no effort to comprehend the emotional needs of others, including their children. Living with emotionally immature people is difficult due to their poor receptive capacity; they want you to offer solutions, but they won't accept them.

Four Types of Emotionally Immature Parents.

There are four categories of emotionally immature parents: emotionally immature, driven, passive, and rejecting. They do not know how to be emotionally available to their children because they are all self-centered and self-absorbed. They all lack empathy, making it difficult to establish rapport with them. They leave others feeling depleted. They are terrified of expressing their genuine emotions and seek solace in controlling others.

Their children think they are emotionally invincible because they are emotionally unavailable. They are miserable in interpersonal interactions.

Key Element

The four categories of emotionally immature parents are narcissistic, self-centered, and emotionally unreliable.

Emotionally immature parents: Use their children to feel better, thus burdening their children with adult issues.

Cannot view their various children as distinct individuals; instead, they view them through the lens of their own parental needs.

Have children whose needs are subsumed by those of their parents, resulting in a loss of self-awareness.

How Various Children Respond to Emotionally Immature Parenting.

How children respond to their parent's emotional immaturity varies. They generate subconscious healing fantasies regarding how the situation would improve.

If children are aware that their true selves are not accepted, they will develop a role-self to maintain their status as valuable family members. Healing fantasies provide children with hope for a prosperous future. When emotionally immature parents raise children, they develop externalizing or internalizing skills. Internalizers believe the solution lies within, whereas externalizers believe the key lies. This indicates that internalizers are prone to experiencing inner distress.

Key Element

All emotionally deprived children develop a healing fantasy to make life what it's meant to be for them. Coping strategies cause the true child to hide within the family. Successful marital therapy is required to help people realize that they are trying to force their partners to have the sweet childhood they were denied.

How It Feels to Be an Internationalized

All internalizers are extraordinarily perceptive and sensitive to others. They have a strong desire to form relationships with those nearby. They have solid passions but don't want to be a bother, so they are typically emotionally neglected.

For these individuals, their role-self is externally focused, and they create a peculiar healing fantasy that can alter the feelings and attitudes of others. They receive little to no assistance from others and expect little to no help from others because they do not wish to be a burden and because their active minds are capable of coming up with solutions. In their relationships, internalizers easily get burnt out because they don't know when giving from their emotional bank is too much.

Key Element

• Since they are perceptive, internalizers know when they genuinely connect with others. Due to their intense emotions, the impact of having emotionally immature parents is devastating. When internalizers are told they have a behavioral problem, they receive the message that their nature is the problem.

They read people to ensure that a connection is being made. They believe they will earn affection if they conceal their emotions while assisting their parents. They think the price of love and relationship is putting others before themselves and treating them as more important. They possess solid instincts for authentic emotional engagement. This is an instinct that all mammals, including humans, have and require.

Breaking Down and Awakening

Your true self desires to be known, grow, and reveal its true nature while seeking your expansion. It also likes your acceptance. The true self will always find a way to emerge, regardless of how well we play our self-roles and fulfill our healing fantasies. Some individuals have learned to conceal their true selves no matter how hard it tries to emerge.

The disadvantage of this is that they may develop psychological symptoms. It is not an exaggeration to say that facing and expressing your true self can be disorienting. As panic, depression, anger, and other intense emotions begin to surface, you may initially feel like you're about to collapse. Consider this an indication of awakening to nutritional values and improved self-care. As long as you decide to address your emotional issues from childhood, you will discover your strength. This will give you the confidence to be yourself and live your authentic life.

Emotional turmoil is a sign that it is becoming challenging to remain emotionally unconscious and that we are about to discover our true selves, which lie beneath our healing fantasies.

Key Element

The true self is who we indeed are at our core. It is accurate because it is not affected by external forces or factors.

The authentic self is what guides individuals toward proper functioning and optimal energy. It is beneficial to concentrate on solutions rather than problems.

A breakdown occurs when the pain of healing fantasies and living as role selves outweighs any potential advantages.

When the true self is exhausted from role-playing, the individual is typically awakened by unexpected emotions or emotional signs.

● Internalists neglect their health and rest and ignore signs of pain and fatigue because they believe they are expected to fix everything.

How to Avoid Falling Prey to a Socially Inept Parent

Every child is meant to be dependent on their parents, just as infants are designed to be. This phenomenon includes a desire for their attention, affection, and love.

Adopting a maturity-awareness strategy is effective for dealing with an emotionally immature parent or anyone who resembles or acts like one. Rather than establishing a relationship with your parents, you must first establish an objective rapport with them. Before you build a relationship with your parents, you must determine their level of maturity.

Key Element

To achieve emotional independence, you must determine whether or not both of your parents are emotionally immature.

● To deal with an emotionally immature parent (or both parents, as the case may be), it is possible to gain independence and emotional immaturity. They are dispassionate observation, maturity awareness, and the abandonment of one's former role self.

How It Feels to Live Without Roles and Dreams

Typically, children of emotionally immature parents have a role self that seeks to please their parents at the expense of their thoughts and feelings. If you have learned to reject yourself because of a critical inner voice that wants you to be perfect, it is possible to reclaim your true self and let go of others' inhibitions. Recognize yourself. This implies that you assert your independence, be who you are, and take yourself into account (rather than ignoring yourself) when taking action or making decisions. Take the time you need to grieve for everything you've lost (due to your type of parents). You must also practice self-compassion and engage in self-care. This implies that you must stop giving more than usual or overextending yourself when it's not required. You do not need to have excessive empathy for others. When you think about yourself, you'll discover that your parents will respect your boundaries because you're no longer dependent on their acceptance and love and are honest with them without expecting them to change.

Key Element

If you grew up with an emotionally immature parent, you might fear your uniqueness because this represents a threat to that parent.

Internalized children suppress their enthusiasm, spontaneity, uninhabited affection, anger, pain, loss, grief, and what they wish to express or feel. They would instead embrace authority submission, self-doubt, physical illness or injury that puts them at the mercy of their parents, stereotypical gender roles, guilt and shame over imperfections, a willingness to listen to their parents complain, and liking what their parents enjoyed.

Parent-voice internalization is how parents teach their children to act against their natural inclinations. This internal voice is a constant inner commentary. The voice resembles your own. This voice can make you feel bad and spread feelings of shame and guilt, so you must silence it.

It would help if you permitted all of your emotions and thoughts without allowing guilt or shame to suffocate you. Do the following if you need to cut off communication with your parents. It may induce guilt and self-doubt, but remember it is for your benefit. This will assist your parents in respecting your boundaries.

• To detach yourself from your parents' influence, you need not maintain a relationship with them. Some people who have lost their parents are still subject to their influence.

How To Identify Emotionally Mature People

There are more effective ways to interact with people that will result in the desired relationship. Instead of falling back on old patterns, use your newly acquired observational skills to connect with the right people.

Key Element

Adult children of emotionally immature parents have difficulty believing that relationships can improve their lives. They believe satisfying relationships do not exist because they fear that if others knew the real them, they would lose interest.

Conclusion

To achieve your life, relationship, and career objectives, you must: it is prudent to undergo the healing process with the appropriate provider if a traumatic event from your childhood disturbs you, triggers intense emotions, or affects your current relationships or ability to form partnerships. How do I know if what has happened to me qualifies as a "trauma?" is one of the most frequently asked follow-up questions to "How do I heal from childhood trauma?" Because we are still developing and have limited mental capacity, childhood events can be extremely puzzling. The ability of a child's brain to comprehend events, context, emotions, and other people's behaviors is severely limited, particularly when it comes to those in positions of authority, such as a primary caregiver or another adult. This explains why it is essential to allow ourselves to recover from childhood wounds that continue to affect our lives today. This book was inspired by a desire to assist individuals in overcoming childhood trauma and moving on to a better, happier life. The book contains valuable worksheets to help you comprehend your emotions, habits, and behavior and nudges to develop a healthier lifestyle. The book includes four chapters, the first of which provides an overview of childhood trauma and its various manifestations so that you can better comprehend your trauma. It concludes by describing how it may be affecting your life. The book consists of worksheets for the development and recovery from childhood trauma.

Please leave a review if you've found this helpful healing book.